Mighty Machines

DUMP TRUCKS
and other
BIG MACHINES

Ian Graham

FIREFLY BOOKS

A FIREFLY BOOK

Published by Firefly Books Ltd. 2016

Copyright © 2008 QEB Publishing, Inc.

First printing

Publisher Cataloging-in-Publication Data (U.S.)

A CIP record for this title is available from the Library of Congress

Library and Archives Canada Cataloguing in Publication

A CIP record for this title is available from Library and Archives Canada

Published in the United States by
Firefly Books (U.S.) Inc.
P.O. Box 1338, Ellicott Station
Buffalo, New York 14205

Published in Canada by
Firefly Books Ltd.
50 Staples Avenue, Unit 1
Richmond Hill, Ontario L4B 0A7

Printed in China

Author Ian Graham
Designers Phil and Traci Morash
Editor Paul Manning
Picture Researcher Claudia Tate

Publisher Steve Evans
Creative Director Zeta Davies

Words in **bold** can be found in the glossary on page 23.

Contents

What is a dump truck?

Dump **trucks**, excavators, front loaders, and bulldozers are all types of **construction** vehicles. These big machines help to build roads, bridges, tunnels and tall buildings.

Some construction vehicles carry materials for building. Others have tools for digging, lifting and pushing.

These two excavators are being carried to work on the back of a transporter.

The huge back section of this dump truck can carry up to 150 tons of dirt and rubble.

785B

Excavators

Excavators work by pushing a metal **bucket** into the ground so that it fills up with dirt.

digging bucket

In one day, the biggest excavator in the world can dig a hole that is 60 feet deep!

Big metal teeth on the front of the digging bucket help to break up the ground.

This vehicle is a **backhoe**. It has a bucket in the back for digging and legs to keep it steady.

driver's cab

Some excavators have **tracks** instead of wheels. Tracks spread the weight and stop the excavator from sinking into soft ground.

tracks

Dump trucks

Before building work can begin on a **construction site**, huge piles of dirt and rubble may need to be shifted. Dump trucks and tipper trucks do this work.

Big trucks also deliver sand, gravel, bricks, and other building materials to the construction site.

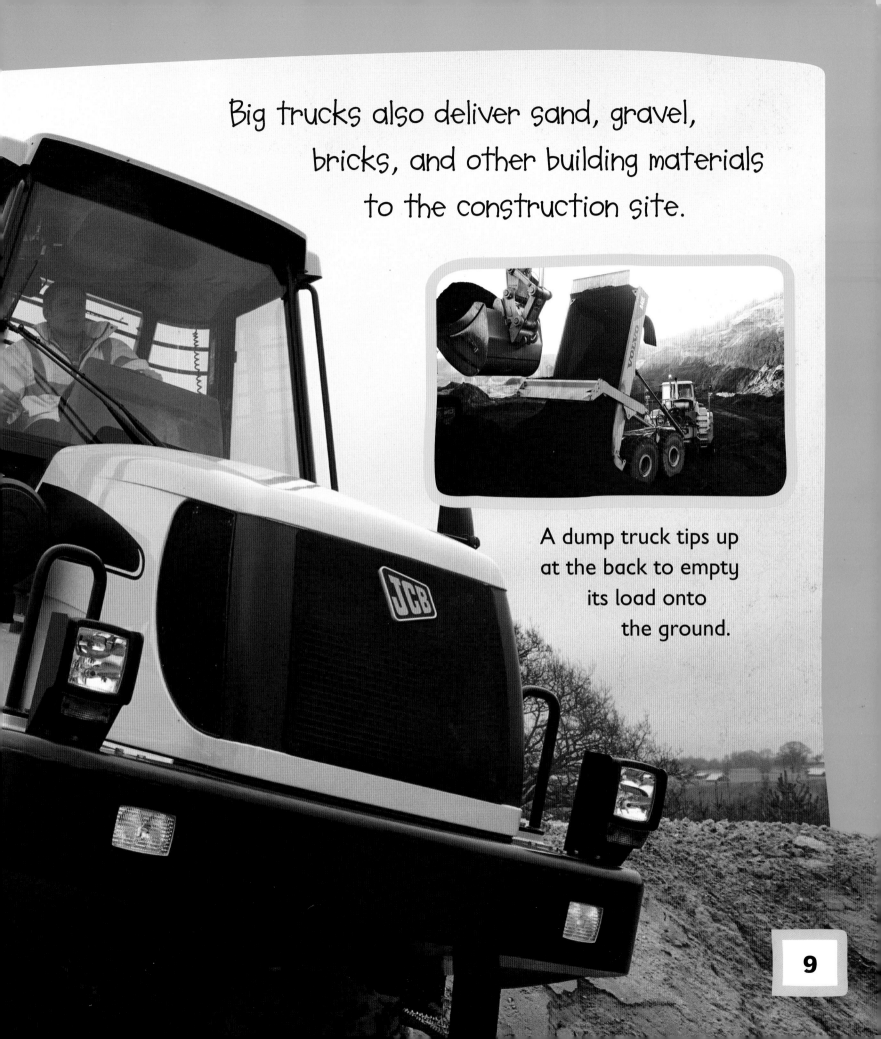

A dump truck tips up at the back to empty its load onto the ground.

Front loaders

It would take a long time to fill a dump truck by hand! A machine called a front loader can do the job much more quickly.

Smaller front loaders are useful
for working in awkward spaces.

A front loader scoops
up dirt in a big, wide
bucket. Then the
bucket is lifted up
over a truck and the
dirt is tipped into it.

As well as filling trucks, a
front loader's powerful arms
can push dirt and rubble along
the ground like a bulldozer.

Cement mixers

Construction work needs a lot of **concrete**. Concrete is made by mixing sand, stones, and cement with water. Once the sloppy mixture has been poured, it sets as hard as a rock.

drum

The drum of a cement mixer truck holds 20 tons of concrete — the weight of 12 mid-sized family cars!

Concrete is brought to construction sites by cement mixer trucks. The concrete is carried in a big drum, which keeps turning to stop the cement from setting hard.

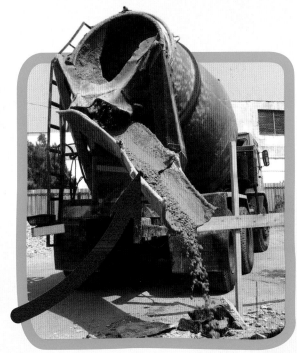

chute

On this cement mixer truck, the drum is emptied by pouring the concrete down a chute in the back.

Bulldozers

Bulldozers are big, powerful machines that are used to move dirt and rubble. A blade at the front of a bulldozer scrapes up the dirt and pushes it along in front.

blade

Bulldozers are used to clear the land to make it ready for building. They can flatten a big area very quickly.

Tracks help a bulldozer to grip the ground, so they can push hard.

tracks

Cranes on wheels

If a tall building is being constructed, materials and other heavy loads may have to be lifted high above the ground.

The **boom** is lowered when the crane is moving.

boom

On big construction sites, tall cranes are kept busy all the time. On smaller sites, special **mobile** cranes are brought in when they are needed.

Strong legs called **outriggers** stop the crane from tipping over.

outrigger →

Road builders

Before a road can be built, the ground has
to be made very flat. Bulldozers and machines
called scrapers and graders
are used to flatten the area.

A grader scrapes a blade
along the ground to
smooth out the bumps.

Then vehicles called paving machines, or pavers, can get to work.

To make the surface of a road, a paving machine uses a mixture of stones and hot, sticky **tar**.

blade

Tunnelers

If a road or railroad has to cross a river or a hill, the quickest way is often to dig a tunnel under it.

Long, underground tunnels are made by tunnel-boring machines. These rock-eating monsters cut their way through solid rock like long, metal worms.

A tunnel-boring machine can carve out 65 feet of finished tunnel a day.

The huge cutting head of this tunnel borer spins around to cut through rock and dirt.

cutting head

Activities

- Here are two construction vehicles from the book. Can you remember which jobs they do?

- If you had to build a house, which construction vehicles would you need, and why?

- Make a drawing of your favorite construction vehicle. What sort of vehicle is it? What color is it? Where is it? What is it doing? Who is driving it?

- Which of these pictures shows an excavator?

Glossary

Backhoe
A digging machine that works by pulling a bucket through the ground.

Boom
The main arm of a crane, which is also called the jib.

Bucket
The part of a digging machine that scoops dirt out of the ground.

Concrete
A mixture of sand, stones, cement and water that sets hard. It is used to make buildings.

Construction
Another word for building something.

Construction site
A place where building work is done.

Mobile
Able to move from place to place.

Outrigger
A part that sticks out from the side of a construction machine to make it steadier or stop it from tipping over.

Tar
A thick, black, oily, sticky liquid used to make the surface of a road.

Tracks
Metal belts used by bulldozers and some other construction vehicles instead of wheels to spread the weight and stop them from sinking into soft ground.

Truck
A big road or construction vehicle used for moving heavy loads.

Index